The Existant
A Cosmological Prose Poem

By
Gary Allen Wake
1958

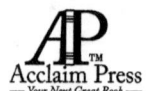

Acclaim Press™
— Your Next Great Book —

P.O. Box 238
Morley, MO 63767
(573) 472-9800
www.acclaimpress.com

ISBN: 978-1-948901-30-7 | 1-948901-30-7

First Printing 2025
Printed in the United States of America
10 9 8 7 6 5 4 3 2 1

This publication was produced using available information.
The publisher regrets it cannot assume responsibility for errors or omissions.

Contents

Prologue 6

Cities 17

So We'll Go Together. 18

The Time of Dying. 19

New Orleans 21

From The Shadows. 22

Parable of The Solitary Spirit 23

Old Man. 25

The Seafarer 26

There's No One Around Any More 27

Who? 28

Song of The Wanderer 29

About the Author. 32

It is said that there was a time
when there were no men . . .
That we slowly came to be,
that we emerged into the order of things,
a product of that order,
a minded-something out of a mindless chaos . . .
That we did not thrust ourselves into being,
but simply awoke one morning
and were here . . .
That we are part of an emerging order,
a vast, mindless system of comings and goings
in a roulette-wheel universe.

. . . but the same fantastic energies
roaring in the hearts of suns,
are flickering persistently within ourselves.

Prologue

I am the existant, the lonely one,
a wanderer among the doorsteps of life's longing.
Endlessly I seek the light,
but I journey ever in darkness.

I am the existant, the solitary one.
Mine is a story deeper and more profound
than man is yet able to comprehend,
for mine is a story of man,
and his encounter with existence,
and his search for truth.
In my wanderings and my contemplations,
in my nocturnal sojourns into the abyss,
I have known the truths of existence.
These I now utter,
and hope for a day and a time
when there will be ears to hear my voice.

There is no true communion, all men walk alone . . .
This is the first truth
I discovered in my travels.
Man is ever a separate entity,
never can he completely suffuse his essence
or intertwine his being with another.

The only reality is found in man,
in his struggle with existence,
and in his association with the others.

This is the second truth.
Man finds himself alone,
on a dark planet,
in a cold, indifferent universe.
His struggle for life,
facing the ultimate finality of death,
constitutes the first and basic concept of his reality.

His association with the others
is the secondary and more abstract reality.
Here, man finds love and hate
and all that lies between.

To seek the love beyond love,
and a hate beyond hate is my task.
I am plagued and bewitched by all that lies beyond.
From the mountains I seek wings
that I might soar ever higher . . . ever beyond!

1

Sorrow is emptiness
and joy is fullness—
they do not exist,
one without the other.

One must know life's deep hurts,
and be buoyed up by her joys and pleasures;
One must voyage the terrible depths
of her greatest depression,
and soar the heights of her wildest ecstasy
before he can truthfully say:
"I have been touched by life,
my breath is life's breath,
and my tears, her tears."

2

I am the wind
that creeps silently through the night.
I am also the night,
through which the silent wind creeps.
The wind of myself
creeps through the darkness of my soul,
and I sing a night wind song.
I am man, the existant.

I am the tide
that rolls the oceans of my soul.
I am a storm
unto my own calm.

Does not the calm contain the storm,
and the storm spend itself
within the enfolds of the calm?
Just as life and all else is contained
in the womb-like silences of the universe . . .

I seek the silent places
that I might fill them with my song.
But are there not songs
which cannot be contained by any silence,
and are there not great silences
which no song can fill . . . ?

I seek the silent places
that I might fill them with my silence,
and myself be filled with a greater silence,
for I am man . . . the silent one,
my spirit moves across the face of the deep.

3

The universe is still and silent,
an awesome timelessness fills the void.
The slow, ethereal winds of space blow,
and touch no living thing.
All is quiet,
and time is encompassed by infinity.

I sit on my mountain in the darkness,
in the numbing silence,

and sense the chilled winds
blowing slowly through the universe . . .
I sit in my aloneness,
and wonder at the starry emptiness
of the night.
I am the Godless one . . .
the people dance in the village far below.

4

I am as the shadows,
my nature is a shadow's nature,
unperceivable in a sea of darkness.
Before a shadow can be discerned
there first must be a strong light,
and I am as a light
unto my own darkness.
I give only the means to the light,
that you might take,
and know that which is shadow within yourselves.

I stand high
atop the old ruins,
in the penumbric silence of pre-dawn,
beyond the shadow of time,
beyond the reach of her lecherous caresses,
and project toward that
which is ever future . . . ever distant,
my voice penetrates deep into the void.

5

On my brow is carved the cruel,
twisted mark of genius.
In my breast swells
a great symphony of creation.
My spirit is flung far,
across oceans and mountain peaks,
and I move among the stars.
Yea, even unto myself,
in the depths of my being
burn the insatiate fires of creation

My longing mounts high,
born by the winds of my deepest melancholy
and I stand alone and sigh—
a creature of the heights—
seeking the ever higher,
for I am man, the existant, the creator.

Man is limited by the confines of his being:
Yet deep within his being
lies the means to his greater freedom—
the focus of all forces
emanating from within and from without—
the womb from whence will spring forth
great winged thoughts,
to laugh
at the nocturnal mysteries of the universe,
at the great puzzle
of all-encompassing nothingness . . .

6

Man created God in his own image:
This is the most difficult truth, the most occult.
When you can comprehend this in its fullest
then shall you be ready for higher things . . .
then shall you be ready for the emancipation of man.

Man has within him a transcendent quality,
his God-self,
a great longing for that which is beyond.
Man has personified and idealized his God-image,
he has sanctified it and placed it outside himself,
yea, beyond himself,
unto the vastness of the ultimate.
Couched in those empyreal reaches
he has wrought the chains of his own bondage,
he has rendered himself subservient
to the ideal of his own making . . .

Man gazed into the depths of chaotic infinity,
looked with bewilderment at his existence,
then, out of fear and awe . . . created God.

In his temples I saw man bent
to his "higher ideal."
A spirit recoiled within myself saying,
"These are not men,
but cattle being led to slaughter.
Like the herd
they are driven by the voice of their master."
I said to them in strong voice,

"Man is the master,
he is the creator and not the created.
Sow your seeds unto the fertile grounds of yourselves
and you shall reap the secrets of eternity."

"Seek your higher ideals,
but not to worship or become subservient to them,
rather to attain them as your higher selves,
and then to transcend even that which you sought,
for therein truly lies man . . . the transcendent."
I am man, the existant, the transcendent one.

7

I am the creator, the destroyer of gods,
the iconoclast of heaven,
the prophet of man's emancipation.

Mark well my words,
for I bear the spark that will inflame men's minds.
The sails of the ships of man
cannot contain the fury of my winds.
The terrible storm within my being, unleashed,
will swell his sails until they shred,
and flap and babble in moronic song,
in frenzied dance,
to the intense, mind-rending music of my winds,
as I whirl those frail ships
to the brink of drunken, uncomprehending dementia . . .

8

By willing does man achieve his most essential defini-
tion:
This is the most personal truth,
the most feared,
the most assertive and free,
... for this only is to be.

An emancipated man, liberated
by a joyous surge of his own will
is a freedom thing.
He sings a freedom song,
a song of himself, of his life-willing,
a song of the attainment of his God-self ...

Man alone in the universe
can look into the depths and say "I am,
and I will to be."
Only he can stand alone in the night,
and softly weep, and boldly laugh,
with the realization of his existence.

I am the emancipated one,
singing my night song,
my freedom song,
awaiting no dawn ...

9

I walk out into the night,
leaving far behind me the towns and temples of men,

and the lights and noise of their revelry.
Outside the town I pause on a hill, and look back
toward the now distant lights,
the sounds faintly and occasionally audible,
slowly, indistinctly rising and falling,
accenting the stillness.

My heart is filled with a gentle compassion,
a remorseful ache for those, my brothers . . .
and a tear finds its way down my cheek.
I turn to go, and my spirit finds solace
in the cool, soothing quiet,
and I once again sense the chilled winds
blowing slowing through the universe,
and feel the aloneness
that comes with the darkest night.

The horizon, that vague, distant line
separating heaven and earth,
seems strangely indistinct.
In my nocturnal blindness,
the scattered lights of earth and sky
are as one,
and share the same darkness.
The darkness within myself merges
with the eternal night . . .

10

Darkness is the great container of all,
light is merely an occasional occurrence,

a faint, struggling brilliance,
soon to be swallowed,
and the night rules as ever before
in splendorous silence . . .

I wander slowly, aimlessly,
into the deep,
devoured by a creeping, inevitable madness . . .

An old man
(is age the condition for wisdom?)
once said to me,
"there's nothing so splendid,
fine and fully round,
that does not alter
and become less so,
for that which comes
must change, and one day go,
and that which glows
in the fullness of its own bright day
is met in time's own devious turn . . .
is dimmed, and cast away."

Cities

Cities are steel and concrete things
bound by wires,
where forgotten architects
piled high their dreams of mortar and stone,
and fathers punched their epitaphs
on the absent-minded time card of eternity;

Where Christian soldiers
beat honky-tonk tunes on street corners
. . . for bread-crumb sinners,
and where gaslights glare obscene defiance
at too-intrusive nights.

So We'll Go Together

So we'll go together,
among the days
and down into the nights,
along the time-worn paths
of lonely men and women,
stealing softly away,
to whisper eternal questions
and wonder at the night.

So we'll go together,
into the morning of sun and wind,
and laugh at life
through tear-stained eyes,
and search for its realness in each other,
and live the eternity of our moment.
No longer will we seek escape,
for there's so little time,
for there's so little time . . .

The Time of Dying

I. Voices:

Now is the time of dying,
time at last to heed
the voices,
long suppressed, long ignored,
calling from the future . . .
once from afar,
now drawing closer, ever closer
with the accelerated passage of days.

Only yesterday I was young,
the voices were still then,
inaudible murmurs,
muffled from within by the stuffing of youth and life,
which has since,
with the passage of so many things,
turned to liquid, and slowly drained away.
Now the voices boom from within as from without,
resounding through empty caverns.
Death has come first from within . . .

Now is the time of dying,
time at last to heed the voices,
time at last to make the journey—
the long journey to the sea,
to the place of dying . . .

II. The Sea:

It was night as I crossed the last hill.
From the crest,
in the gathering dusklight,
the wastelight left by the day,
I could see the dark waters
stretching vast and deep,
touching the darkening sky.
I could hear the roar of breakers,
smashing whitecapped
against black-rocked cliffs,
and a chill descended slowly upon me
as I started down the hill to the sea.

Returning once again
to the womb and grave of all things living,
drawing away from the storm of lives and events
which shapes man's destiny,
which spins his ship ever nearer to the brink
of dancing shadows . . .
changing, shifting,
merging at last
into the rythmic darkness of eternity . . .

New Orleans

In New Orleans old men
     sit in doorways
and stare at nothingness,
      unblinking.
Fresh morning sunlight
and pink, pubescent faces
     add notes of vibrant youth
along rain-washed streets—
     old brick avenues
of half forgotten memories.

From The Shadows

I was there when all was steamy and new,
and dark,
and ignorantly primeval,
when life, in its swampy essence
squirmed and teemed in warm mud . . .
restless.

I was there when man rose up
and waded ashore, dripping wet,
and cowered fearfully in caves,
trembling,
afraid,
ignorant of himself.

I watched as man made fire,
and he danced round fires
in naked,
primordial,
innocence,
and worshiped the darkness . . .
to keep it away.

And from the shadows
there came a chilling silence,
as deep as the ages.

Parable of The Solitary Spirit

One night as I sat introspectively atop the loneliest mountain, my solitary spirit came forth and addressed me thus: "Oh earth-bound one, why do you maintain your lonely vigil into the night, and sit here in the stillness longing for that which you cannot know? The things you seek are not to be found among the heights . . . but among the lowlands. Go therefore, return to the lowlands and be content with what you find there, for that is all you require."

Whereupon I answered him saying, "do you not remember that it was this very earth-bound nature that gave you birth? Do you not recall that it was my thoughts that gave you wings that you might fly? You were spawned in the lowlands, it was my sickness and great disgust that gave you being and sent you forth into these icy realms of solitude."

After a long silence my solitary spirit replied: "Your nature is my nature, your limitations . . . my springboard; your sadness is my greatest woe and your laughter . . . my joy. Your longing is my beacon through the dark skies, and we are one."

After he had thus spoken, I was filled with a great tenderness and replied: "Your silence is your greatest wisdom, like the stillness of a placid sea you mirror the depths of eternity."

And together we sat atop the loneliest mountain and gazed up unto the stars, far into the night . . .

It was the time of the coming of the lions,
like a great yellow
roaring river they came,
through the tall grass
                    swaying.

Children of the night
fleeing soul-gripped,
through the tall grass
                    praying,

sensing swift,
instinctual foot-pads,
and hot lion-breath
drawing closer
behind them.

Now all is still,
save the rustle of winds
through the tall grass.
Lions feed in the dry heat,
under the burning eye of noon . . .

Old Man

Yesterday I saw an old man,
trudging slowly through the snow,
going where
not even he could know,
warmed only by a tattered longcoat,
and dying embers from within . . .
shuffling slowly,
back to the past.

The Seafarer

I am a seafarer, alone
on a dark sea.
A cry, in the darkness
leaves my lips,
for my lonely spirit
would have a companion.

But when my night cry
has died
vacantly away,
and the stillness has once again
surrounded me,
I sense a laugh, welling deep within
and it bursts from my lips—
a thing born of darkness and danger—
and goes skipping mirthfully
across dangerous waves.

I would be alone on my sea . . .
my spirit would have it so.
A companion could never navigate upon the blackness
of my sea . . .
neither could he grasp nor his mind withstand
the terrible pressures
of my seafaring, nomadic thoughts.

There's No One Around Any More

There's no one around any more,
everyone's gone someplace else.
No one lives here any more,
they've all moved away . . .
some to the future,
some to the past,
no one lives here any more . . .

Who?

Oh angry age of disillusion,
who has heard your cry?
Who has heard your wails of protest,
of wantoness,
your howls of loneliness in the night?

Who has heard the mounting voices of your generations,
the symphonies of chaos,
swelling into mighty vibrattos,
emanating from deep within abysmal foundations,
in waves of discordant unrest?

Song of The Wanderer

I stand on a vast grey plain,
knowing that far behind me lies the sea,
         yet I know it not;
Knowing that far beyond me lie the mountains,
         yet I know them not;
Knowing that far above me stars swim
in a sargasso of time and space,
         yet I know then not;
Knowing that beneath me lies the earth,
and the creatures who dwell upon it,
         yet they know me not,
and I know not the earth
upon which they dwell,
for I am not a dweller among the places of earth,
but a wanderer . . .
and they know not the places of which I wander.

Red light
bright,
blinking,
neon brilliance,
piercing through,
arrow like,
the night.

Passing faces
reflecting red-pallored
emptiness,
slipping silently,
like temporal ghosts,
between birth and death.

~

What does "peace" mean?
... the absence of something,
to be filled with love maybe?
but you can fill peace with anything—
old shoes,
beach pebbles,
night sounds ...

I asked an old man,
who shrugged his shoulders,
and said that he was going to buy
some fruit wine ...
God, he had big feet!

~

That old woman I saw
at the bargain clothes sale last week
died yesterday.
I wonder what will become
of that ugly striped dress she bought?
... isn't that absurd!

over across the hill
little babies
squirm unborn
in warm black-bellies

How much is five billion?
Does anyone know?
Could there be that many of us yet?
I love you
I love you
I love you . . .

About the Author

Gary Allen Wake studied philosophy at the University of Missouri Graduate School.

www.ingramcontent.com/pod-product-compliance
Lightning Source LLC
Chambersburg PA
CBHW070933220526
45468CB00005B/1761